Lost In My Reverie

Anahita Joshi

Ukiyoto Publishing

To my dearest sister, Samaira

Acknowledgment

I want to express my deepest gratitude to my Guru Shri. Dada Bhagwan and Meera Bhagwan for their blessings in my life. I want to thank my father Mr. Ulhas Joshi for his encouragement and faith in me, and my mother Mrs. Yamini Joshi for being my editor and guide.

I extend my sincere thanks to my grandparents Shri. C.K. Joshi and Smt. Usha Joshi and Lt. Shri. C.M. Naidu, Smt.Laxmi Naidu, for their blessings and unconditional love.

I am thankful to my uncle, Mr. Ujjwal Joshi for sharing his insights into poetry writing. A very special thanks to my Aunt, Mukti Masih for being instrumental in manifesting this book.

I want to thank all my teachers for their support and motivation, especially Ms.Sneha H. Ma'am for her guidance and enthusiasm towards my poetry writing.

I am thankful to Pragya Diwakar, my classmate and companion in the initial days of my poetry writing journey.

Contents

Lost In My Reverie

Lost In My Reverie

Off to a world in my wildest dreams,
Amidst the tranquility of my own mind,
Where the queen I am and the subject is me
To the four walls of my imagination, I am confined.

Where my uniqueness is the best quality,
Like an oasis in the middle of a desert,
It quenches my Saudade to be,
Lost again with someone or something unknown
Yet familiar to me.

Galloping on a white mare I am,
Trying to control that restless demon in me,
Struggling to run away, run till it has the ability,
Taking off to spill the rose tint of peace in the sky.

These dreams release down my spine a frisson,
Pulling me into a world of my own creativity,
Let me be lost, forgotten in this fiction,
Let me be lost in my own reverie.

My Inner Calling

For some hidden talent in me, I always kept looking,

My personality and behavior, I always kept bettering
To voice my message in society I always kept toiling,

For the best to approach me soon I always kept
waiting.

Tried my best at everything possible to see,

What is the natural hidden talent in me?
Testing my patience and hiding behind this veil,

Why doesn't it reveal itself to me?

But then the real truth came to my understanding,

To open a door never made for me I was striving,

So, in God, I had faith and waited for some time,

I knew the best would appear at the right time.

Needless to say, God had something planned for me,

And the right time came when I stopped to worry,

Now I have a talent that I never anticipated for me,

Hidden in me for a cause to voice my message and see

For the best to happen at the right time I waited calmly.

Map-Less Path

A sigh without relief,
A push with no force,
With the gleam of hope in my eyes,
I stare at the bright moonless sky.

Given this challenge by the thee,
I take a map-less avenue to discover
No far-away lands, no exquisite stones,
Just the true being of me.

The challenge is onerous,
But the prize is fascinating,
For I know if a path is made,
It leads to a defined destination.

To reach there I am striving,
Again, by letting a sigh without relief,
With a gleam of hope in my eyes,
I continue on this path to finish,
The unfinished task that was given to me.

Chained, But Not To Chains

Tethered to society's expectations,
Why cannot I express my emotions?

Tethered to the barriers of thinking,
My thoughts why are you limiting?

Tethered to the great choices of others,
In my matters why do they bother?

From these rules why am I chained?
Preventing me to be a character I framed.

This fear of disappointing others and failure,
Can't cease me from creating my unique future.

As a fat, skinny, tall, dumb, nerd don't judge me,
Nor can you judge my talent and creativity.

I am no more a puppet in the hands of society,
Let my voice, and my queer behavior upset you
immensely.

From the chains of others' expectations and choices,
I have broken free.
Cannot help being different, I am born unique!
I am born unique!

Just Another Promise

No official papers, no profit no loss,

No signatures, no regret no remorse,

Yet again a deal was signed

Yet again a vow was made,

Just by joining two pinkies,

An unbreakable promise was made.

Be it, small kids,

Be it two adults,

Be it two authorities,

Be it two families.

A promise is what everyone makes,

A promise is what a few keep.

This seven-letter word,

Carry seven distinct emotions.

An oath of protection,

A promise is a description,

Of friendship, of trust, of love, of faith.

As for someone, it means the world,

For promises are made to be kept,

Failing that, they are just empty words.

I Would Still Win

A gush of adrenaline rushed down my spine,
But to my comfort zone, I couldn't confine,
No, I didn't know how the future was designed,
I brought hope along that the victory will be mine.

I still stood stationary with my bow, all erect,
Looking uncheerfully at my future-unpredicted
After recollecting all the memories, I was set,
To even take down the ones I love and respect.

Then out of the blue, it struck me,
That I was up for performing a sin,
Standing against my family to win,
The result of my mistakes I could see.

Oh! What an onerous dilemma I was stuck in,
If I step on the battlefield my army would win,
And calling the war off would prevent sin,
In both situations Krishna, I would win, I would win.

Let's Not Repeat History

The sounds of swords clanking and gun firing,
Reverberated in my mind for a long time
Reminding me of those miserable times
When the only resort for people was praying.

Those memories no one can annihilate
Of constant curfews to wars and scuffles
The cause of all this was revenge and hate.

Citizens were forced to convert to a single religion,
Wars and strikes happened to win over a region.
Scholars of such time, what's the use of your
knowledge,
When you can't stand against diehards of your age?

From those times there is a lesson to be learned,
Our precursors made a big mistake in revenge,
This time Let's usher in a peaceful, nonviolent age.

Dear next generations you are all the same and one,

There must be no revenge and hate between you,

Let's reunite and break the barriers of religion,

Let's turn the world into heaven in the upcoming

eons.

Let's Honor 'Her'

She is beauty, she is strength,

She is nature, she is wealth.

She faces and solves problems quickly,

Similar to untangling her hair, quite easily!

Her rights and freedom she desiderates,

Between men and women, don't discriminate.

For eons, she has been tethered tightly,

Chained to the expectations of society.

Don't take undue advantage of her presence,

If she, nature & the mother of all is gone,

Only the destroyer would be left alone.

Her love, compassion, and care are priceless,

Her devotion is unmatchable, work is flawless.

What to say about her significance,

Without her, the world would be soulless.

It needs fate to be a woman,

So, take pride in being one.

So, let's honor, respect, and praise

Her work and dedication,

To make this world a better place.

You May Believe

O Sakha, how can I accept the end
The annihilation of a whole dynasty,
To be courageous how can I pretend,
To my people from death, I can't defend.

O Madhava, what solace is it to me to know,
That in the end, I would destroy my fellows
And mourn their absence while I dread,
as with remorse my heart would bleed.

O Partha, the truth all-wise seers can see,
Why lament over something inevitable?
Of the non-existent, there is no coming to be,
And of the existent, there is no ceasing to be.

You can hold onto them for eternity, don't believe,
Neither to save them, your forces you can retrieve
But only accept the bitter truth of the life you live,
And that it's the start of a new chapter for them,
In which you will soon meet, Arjun you may believe.

Voices Eternal

We still enjoy listening to their poems,
Their works had brought them fame.

Some were warriors others wrote stories with morals,
Their work for society had made them immortal.

After you are long gone the things that stay behind,
Are the noble works that make you one of a kind.

Help and inspire someone to do right with your
words,
As they will only be left behind after you leave the
world.

The noble work of the people long gone, still
Inspires us to give something to the world
with our talent and skill.

To Bring A Star Down On Earth

As I sat on the grass moving to and fro,
I looked up at the tranquil sky dark blue.

The cricket chirped in the background,
The nightingale sang beautiful sounds.

How serene was the environment there,
Similar to the one in fairy tale.

The stars reminded me of what grandma said,
That every person becomes a star once dead.

If that were a true notion,
Then I so wish to bring one of the stars,
My departed dear back to the earth.

Till We Reunite

Could you freeze time for once,
Let the breeze move motionlessly,
Your absence makes the world seem stone,
There She sat waiting for her love forever gone.

Suddenly a blooming flower wilted into lifeless petals,
Suddenly, she lost him somewhere in the bog,
Suddenly, he retired to his latibule,
Again, I saw Her lost in the memories of someone
gone forever.

She sings the aubade to call him every dawn,
Waiting to join him forever again,
Walk those golden stairs leading to her heaven,
Once again, her missing piece will be filled,
She is awaiting patiently, till they reunite.

World Through My Tiny Lenses

My Engagements In My Village

We passed the lush green meadows
And fed grains to the joyful sparrows.

Then I reached my countryside town,
Here is what I did when I was around.

Smelled the aroma of wetland,
And played games on the sand.

Got drenched in the spring rain,
And enjoyed the sweet sugarcane.

Rode horses and traveled in bullock carts,
Went fishing, and got indulged in art.

Helped grandma with my favorite fritters,
And played with cats and their litters.

I enjoyed playing with friends of my age,
This is all I did when I was in my village.

I Am Friends With A Shadow

That dark black patch is a shadow,
Not mine, but of some other fellow.

I have no shadow because I am a phantom,
All white, scary and lonely, haunting a home.

It is my only friend and my partner,
It is homeless and has no owner.

It plays with me in the light,
It goes into hiding at night.

It scares and spills water on everyone,
It is naughty and different from everyone.

Even if I am a ghost I have some company,
This affirms that no one in the world is lonely.

Book Of Secrets

I wonder if unicorns really exist,
If there is a real 'Good or bad list'?

If there are elves hiding in the trees,
Or mermaids swimming in the seas?

If mothers actually have a sixth sense
Or do centaurs gallop in the forest dense?

If Lilliputians and giants live on islands far away,
Or there are hidden cameras in the school hallway?

You will find all the answers in the Book of Secrets,
Where and when will you find it, is again a secret.

What If I Think Like A Child

What if pyramids were built in the Arctic,
And the whole world was made of plastic,

What if parents went to study in our school,
And countries were under children's rule,

How I wish for a coconut falling on Newton's head
And sleeping in a chocolate castle on a Chocolate
bed,

My imagination is running wild,
Similar to the one in a child's mind.

Children are the most creative,
always cheerful, and positive.

So, start to think like a child
And let your imagination run wild.

Dreams Of Winter Holidays

Amy was again hesitant to leave her bed
There were a lot of chores to be completed

The blanket was the best place to be in
The long winter holidays had already begin

The cackling fire was warming up the room
the holidays fun needs to resume

the cosy robes were all ironed and cleaned
But suddenly the alarm clock chimed

Hot chocolate was kept near the fire hearth
And the date was June the fourth

what a good dream I had
Thought Amy who was a bit sad

She only wished that it was holidays time

But it was already nine

Time to get dressed for school

six months to wait said Amy

until the house is under Christmas season rule

I still have to behave nicely to make it

to good or bad list daily.

Nostalgic Train Journeys

As I sat on the train cabinet seat lonely,
Watching the passengers pass by slowly.

All my childhood memories returned nostalgically,
Of taking trips to the village by train with family.

I recalled how we used to run in the train
compartment,
With strangers' kids how we would mingle in a
moment.

Munching cookies and candies during the whole
journey,
Hanging on bars, and climbing on the top berth like a
monkey.

Glancing out of the windows for the extensive fields,
The lofty mountains, the green valleys, orchards, and
their yields.

Sharing food and stories with other passengers,
Hiding behind mom on seeing ticket collectors.

Oh! How I cherished these childhood times,
Of joyous travels by train every time.

Life Without Electronics

Imagine your life without electronics,
Spending all your day reading comics.

Looking up in dictionaries,
for difficult words in libraries.

Helping mother in fireless cooking,
Or going out on Sundays for fishing.

Spending every weekend lazily,
Playing board games with family.

This time will have its own advantages,
And will also have some disadvantages.

It will teach you to appreciate nature,
And will make the difficult an adventure.

Can you imagine such an odd lifestyle,

living without this inseparable mobile?
This poem was just a small important indication
There's a beautiful world beyond these gadgets,
That seeks your attention and appreciation.

Voice Of Nature

Voice Of Nature

I traveled far to see the blue Auroras,

To stay between the fauna and flora.

Away from the civilizations to know,

The feel of fresh grass moving to and fro.

To live in the woods far into the deep,

With my herd of cows and black sheep.

What makes me happy is the chirping of birds,

even though I can't understand a single word.

Eat fresh fruits and green vegetables,

And Drink the pond water with the animals

I want to spend most of my time in nature,

I am always ready for some new adventure.

I go where the voice of nature calls me,

Away from city life which is very busy.

You may think that I am a nomad or a traveler,

But I do not know who I'm. Am I just a wanderer?

Monsoon

Petrichor distracts me from doing studies,
It spreads a beautiful aroma in the breeze.

It reminds me of all the memories of fun,
Of how in the heavy rain, we used to run.

Rain dresses mother earth with flowers and leaves,
And presents her with a quilt of green dense trees.

Rain brings joy to the face of farmers and children,
As getting wet in water brings pleasure to everyone.

These are the things that monsoon gets along,
I've a list of activities we did which is very long.

I and my friends wait for rain so dearly
Because we wish to have some fun early.

The best time of the year is monsoon,
And I hope this season comes very soon.

She Is A Nature's Admirer

She runs in the lush green meadows,
Plays hide and seek in tree shadows.

Makes her jewelry using flowers,
And in nature spends hours.

Fresh air and petrichor attract her,
Rain and spring breeze brings her pleasure.

Eats fresh fruits and green vegetables,
She drinks the pond water with the animals.

She doesn't stay at home or anywhere confined,
The voice of the wind and fresh air calls her behind.

To the dense forest and the pastures green,
And lakes and rivers with fresh water clean.

She is a nature lover, nature's admirer,
And is the dearest to mother nature.

Creating Heaven On Earth

Far away from here is a tiny island,
With dense forest and golden sand.

It is a beautiful civilized paradise,
People there are polite and nice.

They treat animals and birds nicely,
By behaving with them politely.

They grow plants and respect Mother nature,
Because she will only help them in the future.

They love and respect each other,
And also celebrate their life together.

Despite the great diversity of culture and religion,
There is no sign of conflict and discrimination.

I wish to create a world similar to this lovely place,
Spread love, and peace bringing heaven to our place.

Let's Save These Sea Creatures

The titanic sea looks undeniably exquisite,
When viewed from a height it looks attractive,
But this beauty is displayed on the surface,
The fallacious reality resides underneath this sheath.

The ocean is home to so many sea animals,
That play role in the ecosystem which is so crucial,
But now it has been turned into dump yards for
humans,
By being home to plastic, e-waste, and submarines.

All the waste disposed of in the oceans,
Is destroying the lives of animals of marine,
They misunderstand plastic for food.
Water pollution is similar to fire,
Fatal for them into which they are lured.

This plastic waste thrown on the beaches,
Gets drifted away with water and reaches,
The homes of these poor sea creatures,

Causing harm to the beauty of nature.

These lives are helpless and innocent,
Stopping water pollution is important,
Let's stop dumping waste on beaches,
before an irremediable level reaches.

Let's correct this mistake and prevent water pollution,
By cleaning beaches and removing waste from
oceans,
And not taking advantage of these innocent animals,
Because they may be feeble but are not helpless,
As mother nature is there to punish us, humans,
brutally.

Dreary View Of Twenty-Fifty-Eight

I am a kite

soaring in the sky

which is grey and white

the view from here makes me cry

When I look down

I see the building and trees with branches bare

all coloured black and brown

Under the thick sheet of polluted air

the water bodies are full with dirt

the animals are only visible in the zoos

It will be very hard for even God to convert

This land to green and the water to blue.

Now the matters are still not out of our hands

Let's correct this mistake by not polluting land, water
and air

Otherwise, it will be a big problem to face,

The above scenario will be the view of the year
twenty-fifty-

eight.

My Priceless Little Pleasures

The sun was shining bright up high.
There was no sign of clouds in the sky,

Then suddenly there was lightning,
In the month of November, it was surprising!

It was welcomed by a breeze of cool air,
And with the thunder came the shower,

In a very buoyant mood, I got to see a rainbow,
With the chirping-dancing birds; I was lost in the
show.

I rushed down and got drenched from head to feet,
Ran in the pleasant breeze, and sipped rainwater
sweet.

You might think how crazy I used to get,
But these are the little things in life,
That adds so much joy to my life

Lost Again In My Reverie

Become The Light

To vanquish the darkness be the light,
With the help of your knowledge right.

To someone's hopeless dark life bring some light,
By helping and guiding them to the path right.

Be the light that turns diehards into amenable
persons,
And be the sparkle that helps release stress and
tensions.

Be the light that opens the door to happiness,
Help the poor and needy using your kindness.

I wish to become the same light to serve society,
And illuminate their path with the light of wisdom.

For A While

This worldly life is just a play,
Just enjoy it and from it stay away.

The characters here are busy with worldly lifestyles,
You are just here to enjoy the play for a while.

Don't get engrossed in it or forget your purpose,
This maya is very attractive, so be very cautious.

To attain enlightenment was your promise to thee,
By rising above all illusions and making thy soul free.

Don't waste this life by getting lost in the worldly
lifestyle,
And try to achieve your goal as you are here just for a
while.

Bliss Of Solitariness

It is true that you need friends and family,

To give you support and keep you happy,

Who never let you down and leave you lonely.

Yes! It is true that friends play a crucial role in life,

And meeting new people gives you exposure in life,

That protection, and support are given by the family
in life.

But it is fallacious that being lonely,

Is always worrisome and unhealthy

And is looked at with great pity.

Some people like their own company,

It might sound boring or cowardly,

Such people may seem shy or lonely.

But if you want to discover yourself deeply,

Then you ought to enjoy your company in solitude

No matter how society reacts to you strangely.

To uncover the pearls within, Solitude is bliss.

Lost Again In My Reverie

Where I can dance slowly to the beats of rainwater
dropping
Drift away like water to an unending dead-end,
Flow with the scent of my perfume filling the aura,
With the charm of my beauty, the light of my glow.

Dive deep into the ocean to find,
Utmost beauty of all kinds.
Where in my imaginary city,
I can be lost without a trace easily.

I will make a universe, just as arcane as me,
the gleam in my eyes, like the sun shining.
I'll turn my tears into stars shimmering brightly,
In the sky, as blank as my mind while studying.

Sometimes I let my imagination,
Pull me into a world of my own creativity,
So let me be lost, forgotten in this fiction,
Let me be lost in my own reverie.

About the Author

Anahita Joshi

Anahita Joshi is a 13-year-old budding poet. She picked up poetry writing a year ago and realized her penchant for it. Being a nature lover, her poems initially reflected her appreciation and concern for conserving nature. However, since she turned into a teenager she has been using poetry writing as a subtle tool to express her feelings and experiences in various settings including family, school, peer groups, and society. She feels poetry gives her a space to be vulnerable, unrealistic, and more fully herself.

She enjoys being with her friends, singing, trying her hands in the kitchen, and competing in sports.